The Rainbow

of

Life

*A millennium
celebration of verse.*

*An anthology by
Monty Alexander.*

11. 2. 00

Published By
Saint Comgall's Parish Church
Bangor
County Down
Northern Ireland

Pictures on Front Cover
1. Saint Comgall's Parish Church, Bangor
2. Fishing Boat, Off County Down Coast
3. Farm Scene, County Down
4. Harland and Wolff Shipyard Cranes and
Sirocco Engineering Works, Belfast

Preface

For over one hundred years St. Comgall's Parish Church has stood on a prominent island site in the centre of Bangor. Its lofty spire points to the great creator God and its majestic architecture enables all sorts of people to find hope in life and eternal peace with that God, but a building is not truly a church until it has members. It is the people of God who are the church. It is the word of God preached that gives it its authority.

I am thankful to our heavenly Father that he continues to bring many people of talent and ability within the family of Bangor Parish. Recently Monty Alexander and his family joined us and we soon discovered Monty's talent for writing poetry. When, as a member of the Select Vestry, he offered the proceeds of a book of verse to help liquidate the heavy necessary expenditure on church property we were delighted.

On behalf of the Select Vestry I express our deep gratitude to Monty as well as to those individuals, organisations and businesses who have sponsored a poem or made a donation.

I commend the book with the hope and prayer that it will be well supported and bring pleasure to all who read it.

W. L. Desmond McCreery.

W. L. Desmond McCreery
St. Comgall's Rector
Bangor

ACKNOWLEDGEMENTS

Gratitude and thanks to the Reverend Canon W.L. Desmond McCREERY, B.D. G.O.E., Rector of Saint Comgall's Parish Church, Bangor, the Reverend T. Kyle HANLON, B.A., B.Th., Curate, also Mr John BATEMAN, B.A., Lay Reader, and all the members of the Select Vestry for supporting this publication.

ALSO THANKS TO

Mr James LAVERY of WJL Photography, Bangor, who prepared the various pictures that feature both inside and on the cover of this book. The Very Reverend Charles COMBE, former Dean of Kilmore, Dr William McBRIDE, Mr Victor SLOAN, Mr Grahame FOOTE and Mrs Christine McDOWELL, Parish Administrator, for their support.

SPECIAL THANKS TO

Mr Graham BROWN of In-House Publications, Portadown, for the typesetting and design of this anthology. Also the Sponsors whose financial input was essential for publication.

All proceeds from the sale of this book are for Saint Comgall's Parish Church, Bangor, to help with the cost of repairs to the bell tower and other church property.

ISBN 0 9537418 0 X

Printed by
Northern Whig Ltd., 107 Limestone Road, Belfast.

What a magnificent lead our Churchwarden has given to us all. By dedicating his literary skills to the glory of God and the edification of his Church, he has also succeeded in providing immense pleasure to a wide circle. Congratulations, Monty; we hope the sales go well.. We wish you good luck in the name of the Lord!

It was in the year 1882 that our parish church was consecrated. It was in this year also that another poet committed his thoughts to writing. On the evening of June 6, 1882, George Matheson was inspired to write his well-known hymn: 'O Love that wilt not let me go'. May we, the people of St Comgall's experience that love in ever increasing measures, and may we be enabled, by God's grace, to impart it to others.

J. Charles Combe

(former Dean of Kilmore)

Index

Index

Index

A Brief History Touching The Life of Saint Comgall

When the light of Christianity was all but extinguished by the barbarian hordes sweeping across Europe in the dark ages, it remained alive in Ireland, where it was nurtured by pious men of learning. It was this ember that was destined to rekindle the torch of Christ across a continent devastated by the followers of pagan myths and deities.

It is well know in ecclesiastical circles that Saint Comgall of Bangor, circa 517AD - 601AD stands to the fore among the greatest of Christian Missionary Teachers. With the general populace however he does not seem to have been afforded the pre-eminence of his contemporary Saint Columba, or even that of his greatest disciples, namely Saint Columbanus and Saint Gall. This may be the result of the historical significance given to the 'Iona' settlement of Saint Columba in Scotland. Another factor may be the widespread fame and success of Saint Columbanus, Saint Gall and other Irish missionaries, especially in France, Germany, Switzerland and Italy. It should not be forgotten that this success, stemmed from Saint Comgall and his missionary school at Bangor.

It is an accepted fact that each of our lives affect many others, but the life of Saint Comgall helped to shape the entire world, in thought, deed and allegiance to Christ. His tenacity and strength of purpose has seldom been equalled.

It is believed that Saint Comgall, born at Magheramourne in what is now the County of Antrim, was a Soldier before he became a man of God, having studied under Saint Finnian and others of similar standing. It is said that he was both frugal, austere and well used to great hardship, qualities which he also expected from his followers, in addition to them being students of Christ. This training produced the ideal Crusader in those hard and terrible times.

Ireland became known as 'The Island of Saints and Scholars', through the endeavours of early Irish Clerics such as Saint Comgall.

The first poem in this anthology is simply called 'Saint Comgall', reflecting on the man himself and also the Church that bears his name, 'The Parish Church of Bangor'.

Monty Alexander
18th January 1999

Poem - SAINT COMGALL

On behalf of

(Designers and Manufacturers of Fine Kitchen Furniture)
29 Whiterock Road,
Killinchy,
Co. Down
BT23 6PT
Tel. 028 97 541549

Saint Comgall's Parish Church, Bangor, County Down
from a painting by Miss Winnie McVeigh, Parishioner.

Saint Comgall

In the Isles of the West where cold winds blow,
There dwelt a young soldier a long time ago,
Who lived by the sword, the spear and the bow,
        Then these ways he forsook;
That soldier was Comgall from Antrim's shore,
Blessed with wisdom and vision that opened the door,
To the ways of the Lord in the darkness of yore,
        For truth he'd search and look.

With St Finnian and others he chose to abide,
In whose shadow he listened close by their side,
Laws of Moses and Gospels to him were applied,
        In Comgall they must have been proud;
For his endeavours began in the north of the land,
Where he shone as a light with his following band,
Many more coming forth beside him to stand,
        His message was clear to the crowd.

"Go forth to the heathen, the wicked and wise,
Pass on the Lord's word, worry not of demise,
You're not to be daunted, their souls are the prize",
        And so the message was spread;
From the rolls and the scripts it sounded again,
O'er the mountains, the valleys, lakes and the plain,
The Goth and the Vandal had laboured in vain,
        A passing recalled with dread.

Comgall was divinely blessed, anyone could see,
Men came on his calling and followed his decree,
Passing on his teachings to others o'er the sea,
        Thus the ember became a flame;
In dells and hostile places the truth began to flow,
To barbarian and the pagan they fearlessly did go,
The word of the Nazarene was sowed for it to grow,
        By men who were not tame.

At the fork of two roads in old Bangor Town,
Is the Church of Comgall that Saint of renown,
Proudly built it stands in the County of Down,
        A reminder in our day;
'Twas here that he walked the brow of the hill,
Striving in thought to do and answer God's will,
Directing others with knowledge and skill,
        Them with their part to play.

Gone are fourteen centuries with Comgall in repose,
His story now of legend to reflect on and disclose,
Here in the north-land, his memory glows,
    Where his Church points above;
Celtic Cross on the Spire o'er this Hallowed Hall,
Belfry Bells hung within, to peal and to call,
Come forth to a Pew before his Pulpit tall,
    And hear of Christian love.

Hark to the God of Creation, to him now turn your face;
Know of Abraham, Isaac and Jacob, fathers of our race.
Let the word born in Bethlehem fill you with 'The Grace',
    At Bangor on the hill.

14.1.99

4

The Bushmills to Portrush Hydro-Electric Tramway, built in the 1880s was the first of its kind in the World, an engineering feat by men of talent and vision. It is regrettable that circumstances dictated it had to be closed and dismantled in 1950. Whilst on holiday I waited beside the track for the tram as a child with my parents, and can still remember the thrill of seeing it approach.

Rails of Yesteryear

Around the north corner I'll wander and roam,
Where gale and the gannet skim o'er the foam.
I'll stand where the land falls away to the sea,
With dune and sea-shell between water and me.

Out to the west from whence the wind blows,
Dark Donegal hills where the sun always goes,
Then on one's right at the 'White Rocks' to stare,
Scene to be savoured so splendidly rare.

Head of the Giant his beard on the shore,
Captured in stone with his nose to the fore;
Sea spirits eternal, dance around him with grace,
So always he has a smile on his face.

Caressing his brow they scamper and bound,
Up over the headland, in caves on the ground,
Through the 'Arch of the Wish' like sirens they go,
As waves crash and beat the boulders below.

Retreat of the tide along this wild scene,
Uncovers the winkle where water has been,
Clinging to rocks on which fishermen stand,
Casting lured long lines out from the land.

I remember the Tram that used to run here,
On a track that meant it was easy to steer;
From 'The Port' to 'The Bush' it cantered along,
Clanking iron o'er the rail in rhythmic song.

On hard wooden seats, folk within or without,
The shopper, the worker, tourist looking about;
They gazed at ancient Dunluce in sunshine or rain,
A rugged stone beauty from that little train.

The driver hunched over controls made of brass;
Machine sweeping by clumps of harebell and grass.
This magical scene in my mind I now see,
With dune and sea-shell between water and me.

2.5.98

Poem - THE RAINBOW

On behalf of

Burglar Alarms and Security Systems Fitted.
Domestic, Business and Industrial

188a Rathgael Road,
Bangor
Co. Down

Tel. 028 91 467237
Fax. 028 91 471514/456585

Proprietors: Tom Smyth & Norman Taylor

*Specially written for Betty Nelson's Sunday School Class,
at the Parish Church of Ballantrae, Scotland.*

The Rainbow

The eternal essence of all life, has fallen on the land;
Washing petal, leaf and grass, a picture sharp and grand.
At times a symbol from our God, the Halo does appear;
Entrancing those beholding, by refraction through each tear.

Now Bacon measured the angle, from its zenith to the ground;
Newton counted the colours, in that arch perfect and round.
Each were equally mystified, like the Greeks of long ago;
Whose thoughts did reel in fury, to find why it was so.

The colour Red reminds me, of the Shepherd's sky at night;
And banners of the brave, who stand for what is right.
Orange recalls from memory, fragrance of a warmer clime;
Where Crusader faced the Infidel, in that bygone time.

Yellow is the Whins of spring, or patchwork autumn shades;
That herald the chills of winter, as the summer fades.
Sheen of Green, it is sweet, a blend of plant and tree;
Covering all in glory, the forest, field and lea.

Blue reflects the Artist's brush and Lagoons of a southern sea;
Or the mantle of the morning, as dark corners flee.
Violet that ethereal tone, is also in the fray;
Subtly merging with Indigo in heavenly display.

The Royal tinge of Purple, raises thoughts of 'Patrician Rome';
And those marching Legions, who made the World their home.
Thus this majestic coloured curve, in celestial glowing light;
Has enthralled the mind of man, since the flood petered out of sight.

The Rainbow was ordained by God, to rise where Eagles fly;
Sealing his promise to Noah, no more floods for all to die.
The indispensable nectar of life, now drops as gentle rain;
That Bow in amazing grandeur, to appear, again and again.

20 May 1997

Poem - THE EMIGRANT'S RETURN

On behalf of

Harold R. Alexander and
Dr. Joyce M. Alexander
Pennsylvania, U.S.A

The Emigrant's Return

My eyes took in the gable wall, from beneath the lintel stone;
Pointing stark towards open sky, the tapering chimney cone.

Time worn timbers overhead, exposed by missing thatch;
Forever gone the old half door, with its loose and welcome latch.

Precious memories engulfed me, across the divide of time,
Standing there within those walls, held by sand and lime.

The empty hearth lay cold and bleak, overhung by vacant crook;
Still on the wall a candle sconce, inside the window nook.

Gone the days that light had shone, guiding us on the wave to lee,
Returning home with net and catch, the harvest of the sea.

Along a vortex to the past, my mind did reel and spin,
As I reached across the years, to youth and all my kin.

I saw my Mother sitting, in the shelter of a shawl,
She always wrapped around me, when I was cold and small.

I heard Father call my name, as he laboured at the shore,
And I believe I answered him, like many years before.

Then a movement on the hill, caught the corner of my eye,
'Twas my true love, Dearest Darlin', contoured against the sky.

I ran out to embrace her, whom I left so long ago,
My heart filling with gladness, as I called from there below.

Then I awoke from my daydream, in the shade of the chimney cone;
Standing there in silent witness, I was very much alone.

25.4.97

Poem - The Apprentice

On behalf of

Service Specialists in Volkswagen and Audi
also
All Leading Makes
NN Motors
Unit 8
96 Abbey Street
Bangor
Co Down
BT20 2QT

Tel. 028 91 453368

Proprietor: Mr Noel Mutch

The transition of Schoolboy to Apprentice and then the slow progression to the rank of Tradesman or Journeyman within engineering, was for some an arduous time and truly a learning experience.

The Apprentice

The boy stood tall and scrawny, tow upon his head,
His arms they were not brawny, all confidence had fled.

The engineers glared at him, 'neath each oily brow,
Everywhere dark and grim, no smile did it allow.

Foreman sighted on the floor, cue for some to hammer,
With the thumping din and roar, no need for fancy grammar.

The Boss crooked his finger, brought him to a bench,
Said he, "You're not to linger, there's tools and wrench".

"Start dismantling what you see, I'll watch what you do,
Any problems come to me, your always in my view".

Thus the days of the engineer, began on leaving school,
Machines and metal his career, micrometer and steel rule.

Molten mass of iron poured, the lathe's turning bite,
Tedious technicalities explored, things to get just right.

Cutting of the rolled steel joist, welding of the steel,
Repairs to the raising hoist, calibration of a wheel.

These are things the boy learned, progressing to a man,
Guided by all those concerned, in the engineering plan.

In manhood he stood brawny, cap upon his head,
His arms no longer scrawny, doubts erased and fled.

2.9.98

Poem - THE BIRD SANCTUARY

On behalf of

Ulster Property Sales
88 Main Street
Bangor, Co Down
BT20 4AG
Tel. 028 91 271185
Fax.028 91 461108
Area Director: Mr Ronald McMillan

Ward Park, Bangor, County Down.

The Bird Sanctuary

'Ward Park'

An island raised in the lake,
With birds of every kind,

For resting and to launch from,
Along the bank they're lined.

Some hunkered down in the dust,
Eyes closed with feathers spread,

Coloured brown or lustre green,
Some different shades of red.

A Goose it struts upon the grass,
Head raised in knowing look,

Ignoring other feathered types,
And the swooping rook.

The children whoop and chuckle,
As they spread the bread around,

Birds rush to get their share,
Leaving that island mound.

This haven of tranquillity,
Gives pleasure through each year,

For creatures of the air to nest,
Then younger ones appear.

16.3.97

Poem - SPAWN OF OAK

Dedicated in memory of

Edward John Miley

For his years of devoted service
to St. Comgall's Parish Church
and
6th Bangor Boys Brigade Company

Remembered with love by his family

"The Boys' Brigade Vesper Hymn"

Great God, Who knowest each Boy's need,
Bless Thou our watch, and guard our sleep,
Forgive our sins of thought and deed,
And in Thy peace Thy Servants keep.

We thank Thee for the day that's done,
We trust Thee for the days to be,
Thy love we learn in Christ Thy Son,
O may we all His glory see!

Spawn Of Oak

An acorn fell from a mighty tree
And lay upon the ground;
A tasty morsel for a squirrel to see,
To hide so as to be found.

The squirrel went of to search for more
And a jackdaw entered the plot;
He stuck his head in the squirrel's store,
Stealing the acorn so easy to spot.

The piebald raider soared off with his prize,
A successful thief in full flight;
But with a slip of the beak and anguished cries,
The acorn fell down out of sight.

As the bird circled round, a wandering fawn,
Stepped on the nut where it lay,
A dainty push of a hoof and it was gone,
The magpie barred from the play.

The acorn now in the dark and damp,
Hidden from fur and feather;
Lying unseen by the sun's piercing lamp
And creatures that graze or gather.

Coming of spring then warmed up the soil
And the acorn felt it and woke;
Curled seedling within being told to uncoil,
Then upwards it started to poke.

The life of an Oak had now begun,
Anchored well in the ground;
A sturdy perch for the birds to have fun,
With squirrels running around.

17.2.99

Poem - SHADOWS

On behalf of

Shadows

Shadows here and shadows there,
shadows on the ground,
As the morning sun appears,
shadows all around.

Shadows long and shadows short,
shadows on the wall,
With the emerging gift of light,
shadows for us all.

Shadows streaking everywhere,
shadows o'er the lawn,
Shadows always at their best,
following on the dawn.

To look upon your shadow,
rise early in the morn,
On seeing the segmented sun,
your shadow will be born.

17.4.99

Poem - THE COAST

On behalf of

BOLAND REILLY HOMES LTD

Building Contractors
2 Dunkeld Road Bangor
Co Down
BT19 6RQ
Tel. 028 91 270835
Fax.028 91 458940

The Coast

'Tis an old grey morning overcast
the cloud letting light pass through;
Dare I ask, if this weather's to last,
no chance of a change of view ?

Watching the sea's pulsating sheet,
breathing mountainous mass so alive;
Scavenger birds on rocks at my feet,
I see the lone Cormorant dive.

Ship on the horizon from England's shore,
passes an outlying buoy;
A flock of Gulls, perhaps a score,
hover and plummet with joy.

A ray of sunshine streaks the sky,
to peckers and divers a sign,
To fluff themselves up on rocks that lie,
along this ancient shore line.

A rounded head with pointed snout,
appears through surf and the foam;
Sleek hunter of the deep is about,
patrolling reefs of its watery home.

No need for stores or larders these,
like man preordained to plough;
They reap the bounty of the seas,
to survive on what life will allow.

25.6.98

Poem - AN APPRECIATION OF
ROBERT OWEN AND NEW LANARK

On behalf of

Picture reproduced by kind permission of
New Lanark Conservation Trust

Robert Owen (1771-1858) Reformer and Socialist, born at Newtown, Montgomeryshire, was the son of a Saddler and Ironmonger. He displayed genius at an early age, becoming the Manager of a Manchester Cotton Mill at 19 years old. He later persuaded partners to join with him in the purchase of the New Lanark Mills in Scotland, where he settled pre 1800, as Manager and part owner, marrying the daughter of the previous owner. He thus became responsible for around 2000 workers, whose welfare and that of their families along with education for their children were his great concern. He introduced the first infant school in Great Britain, at New Lanark, a creche and a welfare scheme for those who were sick and unable to work. He also banned the use of young children in the mill and reduced the length of the working day. His endeavours, looked on suspiciously by some of his contemporaries, paid handsome dividends, with the New Lanark Mills thriving. He extended his scheme later in life to America, with the same benevolent principles, but not with success.

His four sons all became American Citizens and the eldest, Robert Dale Owen, served as a Congress Man. He was responsible for many reforms in his adopted country and during his career was appointed to Naples as United States Ambassador.

Robert Owen was a man well ahead of his time and in the years to follow, his system was copied by men of similar ilk, not least in Ulster where the Linen Industry was becoming mechanised, in Mill Villages such as Bessbrook.

The philosophy and practice of Owenism has fascinated the Japanese in modern times, with close parallels to their own 'company system'. Japan now boasts the largest Robert Owen Society in the world.

The following poem has been published in the Lanark Gazette, Scotland.

An Appreciation of Robert Owen and New Lanark

Cascades of water forever falling, at New Lanark on the Clyde,
Where a Spinning Mill was built to last, there on the bank beside;
Impressive are those walls of stone, from when Cotton reigned as King,
Owner and servant answering the call, on hearing the tower bell ring.

Worn granite chiselled square sets, carpet the paths around,
The Mill Race flows its channel deep, dangerous with no sound.
An arch of stone, with keystone proud, a shackle hanging there,
From when rope slings raised heavy loads, suspended in the air.

Corner-stones by the Mason's hand, run from base to roof,
Meant to be no ordinary place, such adornment is the proof;
Built to remain and service give, a monument to those men,
Who chose this exquisite leafy glade, veiled within the glen.

The water wheels on shafts of iron, snug in their slots of rock,
Oh! a mighty torque produced, with transmission to each block;
That still tower up, to the sky, sentinel windows, high and low,
On the banks of the River Clyde, where the oak and sycamore grow.

Iron wrought or cast, forged in fire, festoons each path and green,
Gantries buried in walls of stone, protrude here and there to be seen;
Reminding us of days in yore, when bales were raised aloft,
By the strength of the Labourer, who migrated here from the croft.

The Millworkers Row, haven of home, across the breast of the hill,
Families were reared, nourished and clad, from Mother and Fathers skill.
The Kirk now deserted, once it did thrive, on each Sabbath morn,
Creche and School, with learning for all, stands stark, dark and forlorn.

Inside the Mill, are machines still, the Mules now at their rest,
Reflecting glorious times gone by, when they were the best.
An oil can sits on a window ledge, silhouetted against the sky,
A Mechanic's spanner, abandoned and worn, in a corner to lie.

Iron stanchions stand to each roof, lined like Soldiers on parade,
In those rooms of endeavours past, where cotton yarn was made;
Ceilings curved for added strength, support each floor from below,
Where spinning frames performed their task, erected row by row.

Steam engines of iron, steel, bronze and brass, glitter in haughty display,
From when the rope drive and racing fly wheel, came into the fray;
To drive carding machines and twist the thread, as the spindles turned,
In long wide rooms of dextrous toil, the machinery happily churned.

Oh! Robert Owen your epitaph, has to be your achievement with flair,
Along with love forever enshrined, in your philanthropy and care;
For workers who were nurtured by you, in that secluded hollow,
Contained within a Scottish glen; an example for others to follow.

23.11.97

Specially written for the Northern Ireland Childrens Hospice.

Such Is The Kingdom

Children of God to be recalled
through Heaven's open door,
Lie wide-eyed in innocence,
"Give comfort", prayers implore.

Concerns and trivia in our lives
pale 'neath descending pall;
That humbling mantle's shadow,
brings sorrow to us all.

Small stems of life not to flower,
by each divine decree,
But Christ awaits with open arms,
saying, "Come forth unto me".

18.8.99

Poem - THE TITANIC

On behalf of

Gillian Campbell Estate Agents
64 High Street
Bangor
BT20 5AZ
Tel. 028 91 451111
Fax.028 91 472770

The Titanic - 1912

'For Thomas Clarke'

The Titanic

Lines of rivets, plates of iron, portholes of burnished brass,
Companion-ways, decks of teak, third, second and first class.

Smoke rising from funnels three, although one counted four,
Thrusting blades set at the rear, torque from the engine's core.

To sail upon the briny sea, across the ocean's waste,
A crucible of hope and wealth, forging forth in haste.

The grandest ship ever seen, sculptured metal made to float;
Chiselled bow to cut the wave, path for that mighty boat.

A crystal chandelier just there, above the stairway floor;
The skill of the carver's hand, displayed on every door.

Melodies from bow and string, hung quivering in the air;
All a'rythem Maestros swayed, enchanting listeners there.

Pulsating pride of Belfast Town, beauty laced with power;
Perhaps a folly hidden there, like Babel's fabled tower.

On a course true and straight, it met the ice wall steep;
Then that glorious broken thing, plunged into the deep.

Scattered it lies to this day, decayed by rot and rust;
An island on the ocean bed, for creatures that encrust.

To be remembered evermore, from that awful night;
For the perished and the brave; an eternal burning light.

9.1.99

Poem - THE TIED COTTAGE

On behalf of

Mrs Elizabeth Sinclair
Purdysburn Village,
County Down.

The Tied Cottage

The labourer on his sick bed lay, with heavy heart so worn,
Result of all the ground ploughed and cutting of the corn.
A wife, showing all life's strains, stood by him on that morn,
In the abode allowed to them, where offspring had been born.

Oh! Annie dear, what shall I do? No longer can I toil;
I've done it all, tended beasts and worked the Master's soil.
Everything that was asked of me, from no task did I recoil,
Hardship and foulest weather, did not me deter or foil.

The Master must recall, all the things that I have done,
How I dug the ditches deep, from the Bull I saved his Son.
This ailment truly vexes me, to no longer work or run;
The Physician, he has warned, all labour I must shun.

Lying here I heard the hoof and harness's hollow ring;
I knew from the beat and jangle, the Master it did bring.
He wished me well and called to say, I'm needed in the spring,
And says he if I'm not ready then, another he will bring.

This house is his he reminded me, to do with as he will,
Reserved for the one in his employ, who his broad acres till.
If I return to yoke and rein, he'll see we stay here still,
Otherwise another must steer, the plough and cut the drill.

With his chilling presence gone, I've bravely fought the tear,
My life displayed before me, o'er each bygone year;
Deep the sadness now upon me, but sooth I have no fear,
Reflecting all that's gone before, as to future now I peer.

Dearest wife we must go, despite endeavours of the past,
A faithful servant I have been, but fate our dice has cast;
Servitude is owed no debt and good health does not last,
Our children is our blessing, a worthy wealth and vast.

2.1.98

Poem - A SILVER RIBBON

On behalf of

Alastair Coey Architects

HISTORIC BUILDINGS SPECIALISTS

Carlingford Lough, County Down

A Silver Ribbon

The River flows through green meadows yonder,
From the hillside I gaze and quietly wonder,

About all the past souls who saw it in yore,
Absorbing its beauty and now they're no more.

Was it always so gentle and ever so trim?
Caressing grasses along the bank's brim,

Sweet liquid creation, oh, free running thing,
The sheen on your surface makes my heart sing.

Your depths are a mystery where the fish hide,
And rush beds make way for the swan to abide,

The scampering moor-hen's cackling cluck,
Shatters the silence, disturbing the duck.

Artery of life as you reach to the sea,
The willow tree bows in obeisance to thee,

Without the great water and blessings you bring,
My gaze would be empty, my heart would not sing.

17.2.99

Poem - THE WISE MEN

On behalf of

Essentially Yours

10 High Street
Bangor
Co Down
Tel. 028 91 456789

For Essential Oils, Blended Oils, Fragrant Oils, Oil Burners,
Church Candles, Wind Chimes and Pot Pourri.

The Wise Men

A brilliance burning in the heavens, a star to point the way,

High up in the night sky, guiding the wise to where he lay;

They trekked from a distant land, to the Manger's lighted gloom,

Searching for the 'Christ Child', cradled in that lowly room.

These men of a learned race, paid homage in that place,

Gold, Frankincense and Myrrh, to him of 'Godly Grace';

As Mary held the child to her, she was amazed to see,

People who had travelled far, to meet him who had to be.

Micah's prophesy fulfilled, each marvelled in his mind,

Here the Babe in swaddling clothes, a 'Saviour' for mankind;

The living 'Lamb of God' foretold, in scriptures of the past,

A sacrifice for the sins of man; his role already cast.

The power of God was all around, peace on Earth to bring;

A host of Angels looking down, hailed the new born King.

18.12.98

Poem - CALM
On behalf of

Ailsa Lodge

"Family is our aim, family is our involvement"

Ailsa Lodge Nursing Home,
6 Killaire Avenue,
Carnalea,
Bangor
Co. Down
Tel. 028 91 452225
E-Mail. coleandy@ailsaldg.dnet.co.uk

View from Ailsa Lodge across Belfast Lough

Written after hearing a sermon by Canon Desmond McCreery, Rector of Saint Comgall's Parish Church, Bangor.

Calm

Calm is that time before the morn, with daylight about to begin.
Calm is the quiet of an empty church, far from everyday din.

Calm is the sea before the wild wind, maketh the waters flow.
Calm is the watchful wily old owl, above its kingdom below.

Calm is the burn in a ribbon to run, through the fields of green.
Calm is the bee in perpetual toil, serving its 'Meadow Queen'.

Calm is the sound of foliage disturbed, brushing in the breeze.
Calm is the hawk hovering high, air currents ridden with ease.

Calm are the waves of ripening corn, reflecting summer's glare.
Calm is the foal on unsteady legs, close by its mother mare.

Calm are the primroses all together, on banks below the thorn.
Calm are the caws of rookery crows, at twilight and the morn.

Calm is the heron stalking its prey, motionless ready to strike.
Calm is the fisherman with his lured line, each are so alike.

Calm is the babe in its mother's arms, snug and warm in repose.
Calm is the one on the rocking chair, having a midday doze.

Calm is the silence and still of night, as one reflects the day.
Calm is the mother with chores done, observing her child at play.

Calm are those content in their faith, 'God', to be their guide.
Calm in the belief they're not alone, on this world to abide.

Calm is such hope based on a rock, as the scriptures have said.
Calm was the one upon the 'Cross'; and who for us has bled.

23.6.98

33

Poem - THE PRICE OF PEACE

On behalf of

Mr Norman Hawthorn
Belfast

The Price Of Peace

There's a wrought and ornate gate,
Through a mason's dressed cut wall,
       To a churchyard on a hill in West Tyrone.

Splendid beech trees touch the sky,
And luxuriant yews are lined,
       Giving shelter to a church in West Tyrone.

Gothic windows stained and long,
Let light and song pass through,
       Those walls raised up high in West Tyrone.

Decorated tombstones cut and chased,
Stand within that chosen place,
       Of consecrated ground in West Tyrone.

There's a Soldier's simple marker,
Among that crowded throng,
       On this hillside overlooking West Tyrone.

Beside yonder grave a woman kneels,
Thinking of the child she bore,
       The son she loved and lost in West Tyrone.

Death came not in glorious daring dash,
For him who wore the 'Harp and Crown',
       Now 'neath a sacred sod in West Tyrone.

Unseen was the assassin and the foe,
Of him who now rests there,
       In the shadow of that church in West Tyrone.

The morning light across the land,
Illuminates that crested stone,
       At a churchyard facing east in West Tyrone.

11.5.98

Poem - CASTLE AND CAUSEWAY

On behalf of

E. ALLEN & CO.
Registered Insurance Brokers
16 Donegall Square South, Belfast, BT1 5JF
Tel. 028 90 320439 Fax. 028 90 238608
Independent Financial Advice
Motor, Personal, Commercial, Insurances, Pensions, Unit Trusts, Life Assurance

Carrick-a-Rede Rope Bridge, Causeway Coast, County Antrim.
Pre 1900

Perched on a precipitous coastal outcrop of rock in North Antrim, between the towns of Portrush and Bushmills stands the ruin of Dunluce Castle. It served as a place of sanctuary for many in the past, but for none more able than Sorley Boy Macdonnell, c1505 - 1590; a Scoto-Irish Chieftain in Elizabethan times. A few miles to the east of the Castle is the Giants Causeway, renowned for its unusual hexagonal rock formations, which gave rise to legends of Giants and mighty deeds.

Castle And Causeway

Against an ancient Fortress the north winds blow,
From a mighty ocean where curling currents flow;
A legacy still standing, from our bloodied past,
Defenders of Dunluce long gone, walls built to last.

Here McQuillan, O'Neill and McDonnell all wrought,
Facing newcomers and each other fought;
All now to remain is a grand roofless ruin,
Above the wild sea where its kitchen is strewn.

That is a story that has to be told,
Banquet Hall laid for the brave and the bold;
"Where is the food?" the Chieftain did cry,
"This ale in my belly uneasy does lie".

Unbeknown to all that bellicose throng,
Indulging their stature in saga and song;
Food, kitchen and cooks, had fell to the sea,
As rock of the cliff, became loose and free.

This disaster was witnessed, legend now says,
Through the eyes of a Tinker, from the byways;
Whilst gnawing a bone, on a window nook sill,
Saw the lot disappear as he had his fill.

Place of enchantment to seek and explore,
Room of the fairies, cavern to the sea floor;
The breeze that sweeps and keeps that room clean,
Is Maev Roe's spritely spirit, there and unseen.

The magma when cooled left a monument high,
Hexagonal rocks reaching up to the sky;
A home for the giants, who roamed this north shore,
Not forgotten but gone and spoke of in yore.

Aeons of time read in spewed and built stone,
Recording a history and belligerence sown;
Bringing me here, to where I now stand,
On Nature's great sculpture, rugged and grand.

6.8.98

Poem - WITHOUT TRACE

On behalf of

N&N Cheque Encashment Centre
Cheque Cashing Centre
21 Gray's Hill
Bangor
Tel. 028 91 473 434

N & N Appointed Agent
BCCA Member
For further information call:
Freephone 0800 455006

Without Trace

Paupers resting place of Belfast,
No sign of them above ground,
Reminding us of their poverty past,
Buildings now there to be found.

The 'City Fathers' in wisdom,
Decided they needed the space,
Over those in the Heavenly Kingdom,
Who died without money or grace.

Some claim they never were told,
Saying they didn't know,
As machinery rumbled and rolled,
Above those lying below.

The victims of famine lie side by side,
With those from the cholera plague,
Unlamented, forgotten, there to abide,
From building they didn't renege.

31.3.97

Poem - POWER OF THE WORD IS MIGHTY

On behalf of

your property on the world wide web

PropertyNews
1 Annagh Drive,
Carn Industrial Estate
Portadown
BT63 5RH

Tel. 028 38 355060
Fax. 028 38 336959

Website: www.propertynews.com
E-mail: info@propertynews.com

Power Of The Word Is Mighty

Images transpiring from the rhymer's soul,

Calling on life's passing as years take their toll;

Verse and phrase doth ponder, the glory of the dawn,

Days and deeds of yesteryear, acquaintances long gone;

Life's events and stories told, at any given time,

Likely subjects one and all, for lilting line and rhyme;

A sudden movement of an eye, or a passing cloud,

The blush on a maiden's cheek, another message loud;

Their insight sharp embraces all, enlightening as sunrise,

That beams upon rich and poor, foolish and the wise;

Pen poised they jot away, on what they think and see,

Written words scream at the world, Listen! Listen! to me.

For generations yet to be, their epitaphs not sunk in stone,

Power of the word is mighty, unfettered freely sown.

22.8.98

Poem - ERNE

On behalf of

Billy Brown's Barber Shop

40 Gray's Hill
Bangor
Co Down

Tel. 028 91 469834

Lower Lough Erne, County Fermanagh

Erne

The water lies like a silver sheet, with ripples reflecting the Sun;
Hills descend the shore to meet, as it has been since time begun.

If I were Monet this vision I'd paint, in the 'Impressionist' style;
Like the Fisherman or roving Saint, I have stayed here a while.

Alder and Ash compete for the space, Mallard and Finch you'll find;
Ancient figures of stone with solemn face, on White Island are lined.

Today the frothy mantle of cloud, interferes with the early light;
Quiet the morn; the Heron stands proud, eerie and shadowy sight.

The Pike stirs in its resting place, Trout watch for an early Fly;
A majestic Swan at a steady pace, above them paddles by.

I look at this shore in spring repose, with its floral display so fair;
The Sorrel, Violet and Primrose, woodland carpet beyond compare.

Buds on trees like flecks of green, will soon steal light from the ground;
Shade to rule where blooms have been and plants of the glade abound.

A Bumble Bee raised from winter sleep, explores the roots of a tree;
The Warbler sings and insects creep, in this domain of the free.

Summer comes to supply the need, 'Nature's Table' for all to survive;
Egg-layers in bush, tree and reed, wait on their young to arrive.

The Nut appears along with the Sloe, in time for autumn's chill;
Haw and the Rowan in glorious glow, ensure the Birds their fill.

Cold winds of winter then shall arrive, to subdue all creatures here;
The weak will die and strong survive, devoid of feeling or tear.

And so revolves the wheel of time, as seasons come and go,
But spring is the time of year sublime, here where the Violets grow.

29.3.97

Poem - TRANQUILLITY

On behalf of

Russells of Bangor
4A Holborn Avenue
Bangor
Co Down
BT20 5EH
Tel. 028 91 270303
Fax.028 91 472217

Funeral, Monumental and Wedding Services

Tranquillity

Summer is here, the day is long,
Swift and swallow on the wing;
Land of our Fathers, poem and song,
That 'Harpers' used to sing.

Trees intertwine above the bower,
Where pheasant peck and roam;
A haze of warmth rests at this hour,
O'er the grass I call my home.

Tide in retreat with rocks left bare,
Shell and weed upon the shore;
Gulls skim and hover in the air,
Depths their eyes explore.

Sailboat searching for a breeze,
Bobs silently on the wave;
Standing stones at inlet lees,
Like markers o'er the grave.

The grazing cattle on the hill,
Move slowly as they eat;
Bush and bramble standing still,
In the noontime heat.

Within the order of all things,
Each must play their part;
Adjusting to what each day brings,
In nature's fluent art.

Calmness reigns on land and sea,
No tempest, storm or rain;
Soothing the soul as troubles flee,
Till they return again.

19.7.97

Poem - SNOWDROPS

On behalf of

(Prop. Elizabeth McBurney)

Elizabeth's Florists
13 Hamilton Road
Bangor
Co Down
BT20 4LF

Tel. 028 91 270816

Snowdrops

In sleeping bulbs the ground below,
On darkest days when all is bleak,
Snowdrops sense, 'tis time to grow,
Gems of creation daylight seek.

Forerunners of the coming spring,
Linear leaf hem flowers within,
For all who see, a joy they bring,
Before the Daffodil or Whin.

Perfect blooms of dreamy white,
Overcome dire winter's pall,
In jaded January's shaded light,
All around in clusters small.

They need not the summer's glare,
Of a kinder warmer clime,
Frosted pearls of beauty rare,
Unlike Jasmine, and the Lime.

2.4.99

Poem - LAGAN VALE

On behalf of

Mrs Minnie Emery,
England.

Daughter-in-law of the late

Ernest Heathcote Emery
Mus. D. (Edin.) F.R.C.O.

Parish Organist at Saint Comgall's
1919-1960

House on the Lagan Navigation System. Pre 1900.

The Lagan Navigation System, passing through idyllic surroundings from Belfast to Lisburn and beyond to Lough Neagh, was completed in the second half of the 18th century. It accommodated the passage of heavy laden barges, carrying up to 50 tons or more, at a slow rate, pulled by a large work horse. Eventually motorised barges came on the scene, but the horse was still being used right up to the latter days of the system in the 1950s. The operation was finally eclipsed by the continuing improvements in road transport, with the waterway, its locks and accoutrements, falling into disuse.

Lagan Vale

In a daydream as I pondered,
on a journey I did go,
Wandering by the river bank,
where Lagan waters flow;
White blooms of the Hawthorn,
scenting the morning air,
Bees gathering nature's nectar
waiting there.

I saw a Lighter in midstream,
plodding to its goal,
Laid low in those dark waters,
piled high with coal;
Speed of such ungainly ship,
not taken by the knot,
Negotiating bend and lock,
a crooked course to plot.

Then behold the Bridge of Shaw,
amid the fields of green,
Overlooked by a mansion house,
fit for King or Queen;
Draped canopies of oak leaves,
providing subtle shade,
From the sun's enquiring rays,
till daylight was to fade.

Thus through the mists of time,
one does reel and ramble,
Under the tow'ring beech trees,
beside cascading bramble;
Tranquil breezes lightly blowing,
o'er glazed gleaming water,
Glorious glimmers of the past;
memories that matter.

19.9.98

Poem - SAINT COMGALL'S BELLS

Dedicated to the memory of James McBride (1876-1952), his son Thomas McDowell McBride (1911-1990), and his grandson William James (Jim) McBride (1937-1995) - all lifelong bellringers on the Bangor Parish Church bells
By the McBride family

Three generations of the McBride family ringing together on the Bangor Parish Church bells at Christmas time 1985. From left to right: Simon McBride, Thomas McBride, Jim McBride, Bill McBride. The great-grandchildren of James McBride, Bill and Simon, are still regular ringers in the church tower

Saint Comgall's Bells

The Bells of Saint Comgall are poised and well,
A hundred years old with a story to tell;
The Spire points high and the Church is wide,
The windows stained to the fore and side,
> But the Bells are for all to hear.

They peal on the pull of the sallied rope,
A message to send of joy or in hope;
They dolefully toll with muffled tongue,
They speak to us as the dirge is sung,
> And eagerly welcome each year.

That amalgam of metal, mixed copper and tin,
A beckoning voice to worship within;
That frame of iron in the belfry high,
That garter wheel's turn for the ringing cry,
> To sound o'er Bangor Town.

Give thanks for the Ringers and their past peers,
A band who've laughed and shed a few tears;
Give thanks for the Bells and their musical call,
Give thanks for the Saint who started it all,
> Here in the County of Down.

26.8.99

Northwest

Bitter winds blow o'er the hill and moor,
cut short is winter's day;
A hunter checks both trap and lure,
for creatures there to stray.

That king of flight, the eagle high,
looks down on those below;
Across the land that he must fly,
where rain in rivers flow.

Broken bracken brown, a crumpled mass,
on upward thrust of hill,
From pastures low of well grazed grass,
where cattle had their fill.

Mine eyes traverse this barren scene,
where survival is clarion;
As it awaits spring's emerging green,
with new life here upon.

Balanced in time, nature does sustain,
these things some may ignore;
Larder for all; flesh, foliage and grain,
in God's replenishing store.

12.10.97

Carrickfergus Castle

The Citadel of Fergus, stands on a windswept northern shore,
Where Angle, Scot and Norman, are known from years before;
 In an ancient arch of chiselled stone, above the entrance door,
Are grooves where spears were sharpened, by sentries of yore.

Enemies trapped by portcullises dropped, awaited molten lead,
Scalded, lampooned and blasted by those prancing overhead;
The 'murder hole' served its purpose, until all below were dead,
Those attackers whose fate was sealed, as their life blood fled.

A sanctity of strength at times, or safer outside than within,
Garrison with surrounding assailants, hell-bent on getting in;
Chiefs as 'The Bruce' or 'King John', a dogged siege would begin,
Stubborn, stalwart defenders resisting, as their forms grew thin.

So times there were it could be said, 'twas not the place to be,
Inside those walls, that bastion, on the shore of a northern sea;
Rather than await the sieger's sword, sometimes the wise did flee,
Devoid of goods, but with their lives, to remain abroad and free.

Then there was the doughty 'Dutchman', who landed on the pier,
To rally those swearing allegiance, in that celebrated year;
Cannon ball and musket, had replaced trusted bow and spear,
As that hostile host wended south, conflict again was near.

So when you walk the promenade, wearing woollen scarf and coat,
Beneath those ramparts of destiny, with lapping briny moat;
Reflect on others in the past, who've viewed them from land or boat,
And men who steadfast held those walls, without sustenance or oat.

5.5.97

Poem - Evening Thoughts

On behalf of

UK Automotive Company
of the Year 1999

Sammy Mellon & Sons Ltd

40 Bingham Street, Bangor, Co. Down, N. Ireland BT20 5DN
Tel. 028 91 270444 Fax. 028 91 463332
Web Site: www.mellonhyundai.co.uk

The Mellon Homestead

Photograph reproduced by kind permission of the
Ulster American Folk Park.

Evening Thoughts

I remember long ago beside the warm turf fire,
Father resting in his chair, before he did retire;
Oil lamp with double burner, sitting on the shelf,
High up, out of reach, from someone like myself.

The newspaper it was poised, so as to catch the light,
Enabling him to read it, in a glow that was not bright;
Plug tobacco's heavy fragrance, hung upon the air,
Nowhere I've ever been, does that scene compare.

Griddle, pot and pan, at that hour were all at rest,
For supper, soda farl and pancake, butter of the best.
Then to bed under patchwork quilts, we lay down to sleep;
Before this nightly repose, we'd pray us the Lord to keep.

When grown I walked the loanin, by the dry stone wall,
That far off sad departing, I here now recall;
Mother kissed me on the cheek, a tear within her eye,
A sister trudged beside me, racked by sob and sigh.

Father shook me by the hand; told me to take care,
And remember all of them, I was leaving there;
Aware of my crunching boots, I looked back in final nod,
My future to America, I placed before our God.

Passing the School where I'd been taught, on that far of morn,
I vowed to write to one and all, just there where I was born;
Believing I was on my own, I happened to look round,
The dog he had followed me, padding along the ground.

I patted him upon the head and ordered him back home,
No longer would we hunt and fish, o'er the hills to roam;
He just stopped and stood there, as I disappeared from view,
Never to see each other again; this he somehow knew.

Years have past since I sat, beside the burning turf,
I've seen mountains high, valleys low, and the Pacific's surf;
Here in my adopted land, I have dallied and I've wrought,
Conflict I have faced; I have hunted and I've fought.

But in the gloom of evening, when each day is over,
I see whin bushes blooming; the shamrock and the clover,
Bramble intertwined with thorn, along the lanes of home,
In the land of Erin, from whence I was to roam

23.11.97

The Battle of Inkermann was fought on the 5th November 1854, between a portion of the allied British and French army besieging Sevastopol in the Crimea and a Russian army under Prince Alexander Menshikov. Victory fell to the allies but only through the grit of the ordinary Soldier in fierce hand to hand combat. Inkermann became known as 'A Soldiers' Battle' scarcely to be surpassed in modern history. The allied Commander was Lord RAGLAN (Fitzroy James Henry SOMERSET, 1788-1855), whose wife was Emily Harriet WELLESLEY, daughter of the 3rd Earl of Mornington and niece of the Duke of Wellington. Lord Raglen had lost his right arm at the Battle of Waterloo in 1815. He was promoted to Field Marshall after Inkermann.

But Who Was William Byers?

There's an untended lonely grave, upon a misty mound,
At an elevated Churchyard within the Shire of Down,
Where a sandstone marker, stands proudly on the ground,
A memorial to a warrior from a victory of renown.

'Here lies the body of William Byers who fought at Inkermann',
No time of birth, whence he hailed, or when he passed on.
One asks the question, 'Who was he?' answer if you can.
There's a story hidden here, of him who's gone beyon'.

Did he crouch on the frozen earth, beside the bivouac fire,
With the Crimea's cutting wind, chilling him to the core?
Did he keep watch in darkest night as others did retire,
And recall encounters past, also friends who were no more?

Did he look the Russian in the eye, driving the bayonet deep?
As comrades fell and the front reformed, did he hold the line?
Advancing through the smoke and shell, on that hillside steep,
Did he rally to the Colours, with an enemy to define?

Was he shocked by the dead and the dying, at that bloody scene?
In the aftermath of a battle fought, where victory was the cry;
Did he see the broken bodies there, later smell the gangrene,
And give thanks for being spared, below that Russian sky?

If you must know of William Byers, then think on Inkermann;
The shot and shell, the blood, the smell, picture him there if you can;
To later rest on a misty moun',
Beside a Church in the Shire of Down.

16.9.99

The Highlands

Rain falling down and grey the day,
With cloud there is no shadow,
To the sun, 'come back', we say,
"Kiss mountain top and hollow".

Oh! land of the deer and eagle,
Perennial gorse to live and die;
Oh! land of the scenic and regal,
The tick and tormenting fly.

Damp swirling mist on the moor;
All waiting warmth from above;
The Fox follows delectable spoor,
Of one that he does not love.

An antler forlorn on the heather,
Tool of encounters past;
Nearby an abandoned feather,
Lying where it has been cast.

Summer will rescue and sweep,
The hill, the valley and dell,
For the farmer crops to reap,
Produce for him to sell.

The perpetual circle of life,
Embodied in plant and bone;
The Monarch at rut roars in strife;
Omnipotent he stands alone.

25.10.98

Poem - LEADERS

Dedicated to the memory of

John Gerald Davidson
Ex Superintendent of the Royal Ulster Constabulary

On behalf of his wife and family

Leaders

MOSES   GIDEON

Men of destiny they are born
no doubt divine anointed,

Facing the hazards of each day
opposing those not so appointed.

NELSON   WELLINGTON

At times ridicule is their foe
and jeered at by their peers;

Oh! foolish scorner you beware
for you they have no fears.

GORDON   GARIBALDI

The wilderness has held them
under God's protecting hand,

Their names known, feared, revered
by all in every land.

T ROOSEVELT   DE GAULLE

Walking a path tight and straight
they stand for what is right,

Their epic hour will always come
to lead and oft-times fight.

CHURCHILL

10.11.98

Poem - THE WAIF

On behalf of

599 Avebury Boulevard
Milton Keynes
England MK9 3PG
Telephone 01908 841010 and ask for an information pack
about sponsoring a child

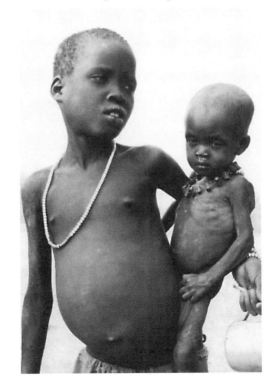

The Waif

Spare a thought for the poorly child
Wherever they may be,
Give freely for that tragic child
at home and o'er the sea.

Neglected mites of this great world,
such plights mar all mankind;
Their minds not on God like some,
but where a meal they'll find.

I see those faces, black and white,
some of a yellow tinge,
To squat and wonder, watch or stare,
from corners where they cringe.

To have enough, is blessed and well
through the famished eye;
Pay heed all ye, who would pass by,
help them before they die.

28.5.99

A Personal View

Monea Castle, County Fermanagh.

The history of Ireland is punctuated by slaughter and counter slaughter, with opposing factions conveniently ignoring, forgetting or failing to teach the excesses of their own kind. Treachery; promises made, only to be broken, with hidden agenda by the participants.

There have been many instances where the besieged faced the dilemma, of whether to resist and fight, or submit on offer of clemency; chose the latter, only to be put to the sword.

One such instance occurred in the year 1580 at Smerwick in the County of Kerry, where a garrison of around 800, mostly Spanish, surrendered on promise of mercy, only to be massacred by troops under the command of Sir Walter Raleigh. Present at that bloody scene was the English Poet, Edmund Spenser c1552-1599, whose revulsion at this atrocity is recorded.

The Irish Rebellion of 1641 saw similar occurrences, one of which took place at Monea Castle in the County of Fermanagh. Besiegers of the Castle who perceived themselves as native Irish, killed all the occupants after reassurances had been made for their safety, on condition that they surrendered.

The identifying factor for such deeds was quite often the perceived religious make-up of each side.

I wrote the poem 'Monea' in the shadow of the Castle itself and some time later on reading it, I decided that it should be foreworded by what I have written here, so as to strike a balance.

Monty Alexander

Monea

The day was cold as the north wind blew,
At the Church I viewed the ancient yew;
Beech, thorn and holly left to right,
Primrose on banks within my sight.

Ahead of me the stones of old Monea,
Roofless and haunted to this day,
By those who refuge there did seek;
The strong, the stalwart and the meek.

One hundred troubled souls in all,
From without they heard the call;
Come forth and we will succour give,
To all of you, that want to live.

Besieged therein, they weighed their plight,
And believed it prudent, not to fight;
The great door then was opened wide,
To that murderous band outside.

Those captives then there met their fate,
Just beyond the Castle gate;
Men, women and children, none were spared,
By rampant slayers well prepared.

Under tow'ring walls above bog and reed,
Encased in time, that awful deed;
Now a lofty eyrie, for raven and rook,
Amongst broken stone and sheltered nook.

27.3.97

Poem - THE GUN

On behalf of

A.S.K. ELECTRICAL LIMITED

Engineers & Contractors, Domestic, Commercial & Industrial
14 Victoria Road, Bangor , BT20 5EX
Tel. 028 91 270308 / 464736
Fax.028 91 458196
E-mail: info@askelectrical.com

War Memorial and Gun in Bangor's Ward Park, County Down.

In Bangor's Ward Park, County Down, stands a German Submarine gun, to commemorate the exploits of Commander, the Hon. Edward Barry Stewart Bingham RN who won the Victoria Cross at the Battle of Jutland on the 31st May 1916. Commander Bingham was a Parishioner of St Comgall's Parish Church, Bangor, Co. Down.
He was rescued from the sea by the German Navy, after his ship HMS Nestor was sunk and remained a prisoner of war until 1918. He later became a Rear Admiral and died at London in 1939.
This poem reflects on the gun itself, circumstances surrounding it and Lieutenant Commander Otto Weddigen of the Imperial German Navy, who inflicted serious losses on the British Royal Navy, whilst in command of submarines. He did not survive the war and perished with his crew in UB29, after having attacked the British Grand Fleet on the 25th March 1915 as it returned to Scapa Flow.

The Gun

A Cannon of Battles long in the past,
Engineered and rifled its death to cast,
Accoutrements missing, with vacant breech,
Quadrants calibrated to measure its reach.

'Twas never meant a trophy to be,
The spoil of war for the foe to see,
Anchored now on its plinth of stone,
Shells on the sea, long since sown.

This naval piece, from U. B. Nineteen,
An iron fish both sleek and mean,
Challenged the might, of the Royal Navy,
From beneath our northern sea,

A Captain of such menace below,
Observed three Cruisers, unaware and slow,
Clearing torpedo tubes at each in turn,
Saw them sink, explode and burn.

Then a day came, no return from the deep,
Commander and crew in eternal sleep;
To serve the Fatherland, never again,
Gone was their anguish, fear and pain.

A worthy tribute to a Bangor son,
Is one formidable, assailant's gun;
Remember those men in conflict cast,
Forever lost in the mist of the past.

26.2.97

65

Light

The rising orb through shimmering cloud,
peeps around the wood of ash.
Above the field as yet unploughed,
wending winds onward dash.

A magpie's nest rocks to and fro,
against brilliant grand backfall;
With morning light moving slow,
shadows dance the garden wall.

The linear foam of eastern sky,
embosses heavenly blue.
Two birds up o'er the hillock fly,
their path within my view.

The sun now raised above the tree,
shines on meadow, plant and dust;
Which the 'Good Book' says we be;
to such, return we must.

Here we cling in Earthly life,
each day under risen sun;
Its rays a celestial searching knife;
Nature's crown, the hours to run.

4.9.97

Vision Of Love

As I rested here outside my door
on a long gone summer's day,
I viewed mountain top to valley floor
where burn waters play.

Faithful dog always at my side,
alert and crouching down,
Watched every nook and leafy hide
with eye of blue and brown.

At that time of year a mild air
meandered o'er the hill,
'Twas then I saw my true love fair,
wild vision the eye to thrill.

Head held high in forthright stride,
hair tousled in the breeze,
Free as the birds on this hillside,
her contours moved with ease.

The golden mane upon her head
glinted in the light,
Pale of face and lips of red
a proud tantalising sight.

Through passing years we grew old,
our offspring free and gone;
Oh! at times I'd see that vision bold,
her skipping along like a fawn.

Snow of life's winter fell on her hair,
frame bent from survival and toil,
But I love her still, resting just there,
at one with the hillside soil.

Her spirit is here, o'er the heather to roam,
as mists cloud my ageing eye,
In the breezes that flow around this home,
until with her I lie.

23.12.97

Poem - MOTHER

On behalf of

Bangor Parish Mothers' Union

Mary Sumner (Nee Haywood)
began Parochial Fellowship in 1876 which was the starting
point of the Mothers' Union

Mother

The babe is born, relief and joy,
Sometimes a girl, sometimes a boy,
Sheltered in a mother's care,
Always loving, hovering there.

A mother's love, the guiding hand,
In every home, in every land,
Uniting all in Christ our Lord,
In understanding and accord.

Close families for you and me,
Across the soil, across the sea,
Bonded by her at the helm,
Under Christ within his realm.

Righteousness taught at her knee,
Keeps you well, keeps you free,
Of dubious things and lazy ways,
All through life in future days.

Her plea in prayer to God above,
For wisdom's gift, for wisdom's love,
So that she'll be clear of strife,
Mother mild and loving wife.

20.9.99

Poem - ON GENETICALLY MODIFIED FOOD

On behalf of

D. BURNS
High Class Quality Butchers and Poulterers
(Champion of Champion Sausage Maker)
112 Abbey Street
Bangor
Co Down
BT20 4JB

Tel. 028 91 270073

On Genetically Modified Food

The balance of nature, what a wonderful thing,
Brings forth the blossom as the birds sing,
And leaves on the trees, burst outward and spread,
In delicate spring when winter has fled.

Producers of honey, buzz along on the wing,
Sweet nectar gleaned to nests they will bring,
Pollen on stamens, they brush and transfer,
Tiny servants of nature toiling with care.

Vegetation's kind kingdom, a host to all life,
Grows in abundance with absence of strife,
A gift from our God, to cover the land,
Now man in his folly has taken a hand.

He says that his tampering, is to meet need;
The wise know it could be connected with greed;
No mind of the creatures, on plants to depend,
Scanning with scopes for genes that will blend.

Through test, trial and theory, variations are sought;
The path that they tread with danger is fraught;
Destroying small beings that fly, creep or crawl,
A new world emerging; a nightmare for all.

2.6.99

Poem - THE SPINNER

On behalf of

Meridian

HAIR BEAUTY TONING SUNBEDS
Fudge Espa Shapers Toning Tables

The SALON that offers the
COMPLETE 'MAKE - OVER' PACKAGE!
Tel. 028 91 271770 or call at 10 Victoria Road Bangor
For appointments and details of monthly offers!

'The Long Hole,' Bangor pre 1900

The Spinner

There's a place in my heart from old Tyrone,
Indelibly held in memory sown.

The spinning frames stood upon the floor,
From wall to wall inside the door;
Each cared for by a maiden fair,
With shoeless feet and plaited hair.

No 'Prima Donna' could compare with these,
Nurturing the bobbins with practised ease;
Sensuous visions for the artist's brush,
Theirs not to dally or to rush.

In aprons of yellow waisted tight,
They watched the spindles left and right;
At times you'd hear one sweetly sing,
The lilting voice a joy to bring.

Lithe movement of both skill and flair,
Unbounded beauty for one to stare;
Curve of bosom above contoured hip,
Blue tint of the eye and ruby lip.

My love was for one with raven hair,
Tied back in abundance, lush and rare;
The blush of cheek and smile on her face,
Made a paradise of that faraway place.

Across the years I can see her still,
Walk the spinning floor within the Mill;
Tending and tying the linen thread,
Mane of hair behind her head.

I've travelled far in growing old,
No longer rash, no longer bold,
And still her grace in my mind's eye,
Clears darkness like a brilliant sky.

19.7.99

Poem - To The 27th

On behalf of

Sir John Gorman CVO CBE MC DL
Ex Irish Guards
Ex District Inspector of the Royal Ulster Constabulary
Assembly Member for North Down

Inniskilling Fusilier and Inniskilling Dragoon on guard at
Enniskillen Town Hall.
Photograph produced by kind permission of the Royal
Inniskilling Fusiliers Museum

At the beginning of the 19th century, between 60% and 70% of the British Infantry were Irish. I focus here on the 27th (Inniskilling) Regiment of Foot, later renamed The Royal Inniskilling Fusiliers. One of their most famous battle honours was gained at Waterloo, in holding the ground at the centre of Wellington's line against a ferocious onslaught at that point, thus thwarting this well proved tactic by Napoleon, to achieve victory. The 27th (Inniskilling) Square at Waterloo was formed by the 1st Battalion consisting of 698 officers and men. Out of this 480 men were lost. The Iron Duke acknowledged their great contribution and it is said that Napoleon commented on their stubbornness.

On the Townhall Tower, Enniskillen, County Fermanagh, are two niches holding statues of an Inniskilling Fusilier and an Inniskilling Dragoon. In this way the town of Enniskillen has honoured these famous regiments, the spawn of its bosom.

To The 27th

Soldiers of stone high up in the wall,
Look down on the Town below,
Forever on guard, proud and so tall,
As years go passing slow.

The Fusilier stands, his gun at rest,
Here in the land of his birth,
Times the foeman put him to the test,
In many a corner of Earth.

To north, south, east and the west,
A renowned soldier was he,
At Waterloo, a 'Square' on the crest,
Facing Napoleon's cavalry.

The 27th, repelled sabre and lance,
were pounded by shot and shell;
That centre held against the advance,
A story for others to tell.

Unbroken 'Square', dead on the ground,
Colours held safe in the killing;
Silent they lay, great praise to sound,
For these men of the Inniskilling.

8.5.99

Poem - ANNO DOMINI MM

On behalf of

Battersea Guest House

Overlooking Bangor Marina and Gardens

Proprietors; John and Rene Brann
47 Queen's Parade
Bangor, Co. Down BT20 3BH
Tel: 028 91 461643

Anno Domini - MM

A moment in eternity, two thousand years have past,
Since the Carpenter was born, a presence made to last.

Child 'Divine' of Heaven's light, revered by wise and King,
Who with lowly Shepherds, homage to him did bring.

Knowing Youth of 'Godly Grace', quizzed teachers of the law,
To astound with wisdom's truth as they stood back in awe.

Guiding the chisel's driven bite and hands around the plane,
He shaped items of that world, never the same again.

The time then came for him to leave, the cutting of the tree,
And begin his Ministry on the shores of Galilee.

As foretold in sacred prophesy, also in the Baptist's cry,
He preached salvation of our God and on him to rely.

His message as a beacon shone, for mankind to believe,
Then jealous hatred intervened with many left to grieve.

But joy emerged from shadow, when he rose from the dead,
Disciples all empowered, his deeds and word to spread.

11.8.99

Poem - THE GIRONA

On behalf of

Down Diving Services
Professional Diving and Marine Service to Industry
96 High Street,
Bangor
Co. Down
BT20 5BB
Tel. 028 91 450831
Fax.028 91 270981
Mobile. 0802 524 104
After Hours. 028 91 771428

The Causeway Coast, County Antrim

The Girona

Beyond western hills, that fiery core,
Disappears once more;
Its golden sword to the heart of me,
Glitters on a placid sea.

Like an arrow to where I stand,
On basalt outcrop from the land,
Where a Spanish ship, proud and tall,
Fell victim to the storm and squall.

Majestic Galleon of a foreign clime,
Fought the tempest in that time;
Riding the waves it searched for lee,
On the unknown cruel sea.

Captain and Sailors, stalwart crew,
Also there, Soldiers too;
Clung to that mighty ship of oak,
As planking sprung and broke.

Cannon and debris, along the shore,
Scattered on the sandy floor;
Broken spars and coils of rope,
Floating there, offered hope.

That ship is here, beneath the wave,
And those men; this their grave;
Oh! sword of light, o'er fickle sea,
Guard them here for eternity.

23.11.97

The Poet

The Bard's mind floats along
Reciting rhyme and full of song,
Attentive to the rustling trees,
Wind caressing in the breeze.

Mindful of each changing scene,
Verse records the fields of green;
World in bloom a splendid place,
Miracle of God's mighty grace.

The seeing words without eyes,
Open the beauty of the skies,
Leaving one to quietly ponder,
Spoken sights here and yonder.

Subtle words in prudence cast,
Become the echoes of our past;
All ye folk, oh, credence give,
Poetic words forever live.

21.8.98

Hughie Linton's Shop

Hughie Linton was a man who dwelt in Belfast Town,
A buyer of antiquities for never more than half-a-crown;
Trading on the Ormeau Road with shop front to the fore,
Stock was from the floor to roof and packed around the door.

Now Hughie dealt in anything that ever came his way,
Hoards of swords and bits of board, were all there on display;
Bird cages and old lamps of brass, to him were all the same,
Utilities, soap or bicycles, buying and selling was his game.

We'd stand and stare at his wares, piled one upon the other,
Retrieving anything within, he had the greatest bother;
'Old Dears' would cry, "Hi Hughie! have you such and such a thing?"
And others for a couple of bob, scrap to him would bring.

Looking back to Hughie, he was a man before his time,
And my fondest admiration is recorded in this rhyme;
Hughie's commodities were 'futures', a genius of my past,
Had I bought all his stock, my wealth would now be vast.

25.5.98

Pieces Of Iron

A Hammer met an Anvil one day,

I've seen you about the Hammer did say.

Yes, I've met you before in the past,

We were introduced by the Shoemaker's Last.

What of the Last, have you seen him about?

Now and again I'd give him a shout.

He's redundant in the old backyard,

And very despondent, he finds it hard.

But what about your brother the Sledge?

Since he broke his shaft, when he missed the wedge.

Oh, he's all right now, you'll find him around,

Either at the forge or there on the ground.

What would you say if we all got together,

To remember old times and have a blether?

25.4.97

Truth

Think not of pride, think not of greed,
Think not of dynasty;
Think only of that sceptred throne,
And Christ in majesty.

Pray for guidance, pray for peace,
Pray ye not for wealth;
Pray only for the helping hand,
And for enduring health.

Toil not in folly, toil not in vain,
Toil in Godly cause;
Toil only for the needs of all,
And exult as you pause.

Pay heed brothers, pay heed sisters,
Pay heed great family;
Pay heed, myriad seed of Abraham,
And note each homily.

There's a place unseen, there is hope,
There will be many to see;
There you'll find the Kingdom of God,
And perfect 'Trinity'.

5.6.99

Poem - AN ISLAND CHURCH OF ERNE

On behalf of

Anita Stuart
Enniskillen,
County Fermanagh.

'For Lassie'

Inishmacsaint ruined Church and Cross.
Lower Lough Erne, County Fermanagh.

An Island Church Of Erne

The rock hewn Cross of Inishmacsaint,
To the west wall of that sacred ruin;
Monument to Christ and the mason quaint,
Dispersed islands around it strewn.

In that windswept watery wilderness,
Some met to worship their God;
That gathering bowed, the Cleric did bless,
As they rested from net and the sod.

Wide walls still stand tall and hoary,
A reminder of times passing slow,
When people heard the Carpenter's story,
In difficult times long ago.

The island like Church now deserted,
No flock to meet there again,
But the ground remains consecrated,
Symbolic for us to maintain.

A stone link with ancestral crusaders,
To establish the faith they did strive,
With unbelievers whilst facing invaders,
Celebrated by those now alive.

27.3.97

Tessie and William Halliday, my aunt and uncle, dwelt for many years in the Townland of Tullyear, near Banbridge, Co Down, in the direction of Rathfriland. Their cottage was beside an ancient earthen fort, the origin of which was lost in antiquity. Its perimeter was marked all round by hazel-nut trees and part of a moat. In the centre of the fort was a very deep well. The place was inhabited with abundant wildlife as well as domestic animals, including hives of honey bees.

The fort, cottage and garden were sheer fascination for many, with tales of fairies and banshees. I can say that it was not just children who believed this folklore, with sounds of the night always making one uneasy.

Tullyear

Scene of enchantment in Old Tullyear,
With hazel trees thick all around,
Cloaking ground where pheasant appear,
And burrowing badgers abound.

Hoot of the owl in quiet of the night,
Bark of the fox on the prowl,
Hen on the roost, frozen with fright,
As Reynard ignores the old owl.

The moon beaming down onto the Rath,
Creates a magical scene,
With fairies arriving along every path,
Some dressed in tunics of green.

Dipping and veering bats on the wing,
Pursuing moth and the fly,
As round the thorn the 'wee folk' sing,
Where big people dare not pry.

Monarch of the unseen, that Fairy Queen,
Presides o'er her subjects all,
But they disappear, no trace to be seen,
When the cockerel maketh his call.

13.5.99

Sacrifice

Wind from the wings of the hovering gun ship,
swept the ground where they lay,

Warriors down prone upon the grass,
to keep the unwanted at bay.

Alert was their stance around and about,
with the slash of breech steel,

Amid the roar of the engine's power,
and crunch of the saracen wheel.

Enemy ready to flee at the end of a wire,
with heart elated and cold,

Pressed the contact as he looked down,
and watched death's mantle unfold.

The beast of the desert lay on its side,
lifted and rolled o'er the ground,

Metal mangled and doors sprung ajar,
echoes the only sound.

Then I awoke with a jump and a start,
in the warmth of the morn,

Far away from the fields of my past,
where limb and flesh were torn.

23.6.98

Poem - A SOLDIER'S LAMENT

On behalf of

The Royal British Legion

Egypt 1944
William Francis Black
of Ballylesson, County Down.

Written specially for The Royal British Legion Womens Section, Northern Ireland Area Conference at Carrickfergus on the 13th February 1999.

The emergence of the British Empire and subsequent military obligations, saw throughout its existence, millions of people employed in the Services, for long periods overseas, especially in Africa and India. Their common bond was pride in their Unit and love of their Country, whether they were Scots, English, Welsh or Irish. Many left these shores as Boy Soldiers or Sailors, to return years later as men. Many never returned, settling elsewhere, or having paid the supreme sacrifice through conflict or disease. The following poem reflects the feelings of one, as he dreams of his native land.

A Soldier's Lament

There's a gem of a Country far to the west,
Where the grass lies green to the shore,
'Tis there my mind wanders, my body at rest,
Recalling youth's ventures of yore,
    And I weep for the land that I love.

I see jagged crags with tumbling shale,
Sheep and cattle grazing along,
The boat on the wave with buffeted sail,
Fiddler, Fifer and Crooner in song,
    And I weep for the land that I love.

I see Swift and the Swallow flit on the wing,
Falling rain and hear the winds roar,
To again brave the cold, that the snows bring;
Oh! to be at home once more,
    And I weep for the land that I love.

I hear the raised lilt of my Mother's voice,
Chiding those younger than me,
I see my Father at toil, in his labours rejoice,
Harvest, meadow, field and lea,
    And I weep for the land that I love.

Here where the Snake and the Scorpion thrive,
And the Sun scorches the skin,
I'll do my best, to serve and survive,
Someday to again see my kin,
    And I weep for the land that I love.

27.10.98

Poem - THE SEA

Dedicated to the memory of

William James Stewart,

Marine Engineer of Belfast and his wife Mary.

Also

William Martin Foster,

Marine Engineer of South Shields, England

'Home is the Sailor, home from sea
and the Hunter home from the hill'

On behalf of

Linda, David, Diana and Ian

The Sea

The Sea, The Sea, the wonderful Sea,
Lashes and washes around you and me,
Moon with the tide, covers the scree,
Foaming white horses, reach for the lee.

The Sea, The Sea, rolling great deep,
Fishermen casting, so as to reap,
Haven for some, to swim or to creep,
Bed for the weed and dolphin to leap.

The Sea, The Sea, grey, green or blue,
Reflections forever, changing its hue,
It has floated the ships, ancient and new,
Sailing the briny, each intrepid crew.

The Sea, The Sea, always just there,
Cauldron of might; what can compare?
Fascination for some, to stand and stare,
Mind on the waters, wind in their hair.

The Sea, The Sea, as onward it goes,
Gathers flotsam, jetsam, dances and flows;
It's beginning and end, nobody knows,
Perhaps on a beach, touching your toes.

25.12.97

Poem - THE PARISH OF DRUMBO

On behalf of

Hylands Developments Ltd.
'Tanglewood'
188 Ballylesson Road
Belfast
BT8 8JU
Tel. & Fax. 028 90 826298
Mobile. 07050 085810

Drumbo Parish Church, Ballylesson, County Down

The Parish Of Drumbo

The Church stands upon the hill,
Where it was meant to be,
Uplifted to the heavens above,
For you and me to see.

As I strolled up the avenue,
To that warm inviting door,
The distant, near forgotten past,
Stirred within my core.

Of times when I was led there,
By my Mother's hand,
With me wide eyed in wonderment,
Bells pealing across the land.

Reflecting round about me,
In that springtime day,
I studied the gnarled twisted trees,
On which I used to play.

The lantern placed within the porch,
To shine forth in the night,
Guiding the faithful to the door,
Like a diamond shining bright.

Oh, sanctity of wood and stone,
You've outlived those in your shadow here,
'Twas in you where they looked in hope,
To God, our Christ and Apostles dear.

13.4.97

For Stuart, Catherine, Phillip and Flynn

Santa-Claus

'Tis Christmas Eve in starry night,
Oncoming sleep the children fight,
They listen for the sleigh bell ring,
Thinking of what it will bring.

They see reindeer prancing in the sky,
As across the heavens they fly,
Pulling Santa-Claus along behind,
Determined every child to find.

Parcels big and parcels small;
Oh! they hope for him to call,
Fulfilling each sought after dream,
With his sleigh and reindeer team.

Bread and milk laid on the floor,
At the hearth which is his door,
To help him on his cheery way,
He cannot wait, he cannot stay.

A job well done before the morn,
Sooty clothes scratched and torn;
He brings happiness and pleasure,
Surprising gifts for each to treasure.

Looking to childhood we remember,
Hopefully longing for December;
As you ponder the past please pause,
To pray for peace and Santa-Claus.

24.12.98

The Belfast Gaol and Courthouse were both built in the 1840s facing each other on opposite sides of the Crumlin Road. A tunnel under the road connected the two buildings for convenience in transferring prisoners in either direction. There were many, both staff and prisoners, who found 'The Tunnel' oppressive and claustrophic. The last prisoners occupied the prison in 1997, and the courthouse closed in 1998. The following poem reflects on these historic buildings.

Justice

In Belfast's sprawl, below Cave Hill, on the Antrim side of town,
You'll find the sloping Circus of Carlisle, in that City of renown;
'Twas just there, in days gone by, that 'Roaring Hanna' stood,
Mounted and froze in sculptured bronze, his dogmatic mood.

Beyond what was to the back of him, the Crumlin Road does lie,
To pass a building on its left, where 'Justice' stands on high;
Proudly raised upon that Greek facade, she's poised in majesty,
Hand uplifted to the heavens, holding scales for all to see.

In those hallowed halls, cloaked advocates, plied their chosen trade,
Shrewdly swaying Judge and Jurymen, with decisions to be made;
Tapering rounded ornate columns, rise from floor to vented roof,
Gilded Lion, Crown and Unicorn, above wigs of those aloof.

Here appeared Felons who flaunted, the laws of this northern land,
Scripted charges there to be answered, in the 'dock' to stand;
As the 'Learned' proceeded with care, at times the accused went free,
Others damned and condemned by evidence, to lose their liberty.

And thus to be led through 'The Tunnel', to Gaol across the road,
That partner of 'Justice' awaiting, part of the punishment code;
Deep and dour were the thoughts of those, taking that sunken route,
Perhaps guilt or innocence of foul crime, no longer in dispute.

Inside that edifice of dressed cut stone, is a double cell of gloom,
Where beings guilty of dark deeds, awaited impending doom;
There they sat with head bowed, forced to contemplate their fate,
Throughout the night and each day, until the hour was late.

Outside that room, they heard the noise, of others within those walls,
Whose lives were grim, but not as theirs, to 'live' inside their stalls.
Slamming doors and clanging heard, of Victorian ironwork overhead,
The hopeless sat, or lay, or stood, future faced with dread.

Prudent watchful Warders impassive sat, through each long ordeal,
The person safe in their keeping, as life the hours did steal.
Unease was rife amongst all there, the 'Reaper' astride that place,
As the condemned, their soul did search, final trial yet to face.

The Cleric prayed on the approach to eight, being the statutory time,
When the 'one' was set to forfeit life, for assumed regretted crime.
With pressure steamtraps clanked and creaked, in those galleries high,
All listening for crash of bolt and trap, as the time drew nigh.

The wheeled wardrobe cunningly pushed aside, revealed a hidden door,
For the 'Subject' to pass through, being ushered across that floor.
Then manoeuvred forth onto the hatch, with hood and loop in place,
Lever pushed and they were gone, to 'eternity' through that space.

The contraption, now dismantled and gone, only flat irons there to see,
On the underside of that deadly floor, where the trapdoor used to be.
Cells have been emptied, no crashing doors, eeriness of the past abides;
In shadowy rooms, across galleries high; where spirits still reside.

14.10.97

Poetry by
HUGH ALEXANDER
(1892 - 1978)

This is a selection of poems written by my late father. He was a natural poet from whom rhyme continually flowed. This gift manifested itself at an early age and the poem 'Ringlin's Dream', was infact written when he was only 14 years of age. He travelled extensively and loved to converse with people being an accomplished linguist. His powers of observation were keen and this is reflected in his poetry along with his great sense of humour. Unfortunately lots of his poems which were recorded are now lost and many more were never recorded at all.

Photograph of Hugh Alexander
taken from his Australian Passport dated 1925

Poem - FAIRIES

for
My mother

Mrs Maureen McClure
to remind her of childhood folklore at Drumshiel,
in the County of Cavan.

From her son - Mervyn

Fairies

The hills of Holy Ireland have palaces inside,

Where snugly in the winter the "little folk" abide.

They come out in the summer when all is fresh and green,

We sometimes hear their music, but they are rarely seen.

For pleasure they go planting, thorn bushes here and there,

To cut them down or touch them the farmers never dare.

For fear the little people might cause them grief and woe,

Or crops might fail to ripen or else refuse to grow.

In raths and haunted places it is unwise to spy,

Upon them at their revels what time the moon is high.

One foolish man who did so found out to his dismay,

That somehow as he watched them a year had passed away.

But they will never harm you or bother you for spite,

If you leave them bread and milk upon the hob at night.

1908

Poem - RINGLIN'S DREAM

On behalf of

Elizabeth Claire Alexander Stewart
(Grand-daughter of the Poet)
her husband Martin and son Flynn

'For Papa'

Ringlin's Dream

Old Ringlin is a country wight,
Well used to sleeping out at night,
The way that he can drink and fight,
        Is awful and surprising;
At Banbridge he got drunk one day,
And in returning lost his way,
To wander far by bog and brae,
        Just as the moon was rising.

He happened soon to wander near,
An ancient fort that's far from here,
Which country men regard in fear,
        For they believe it's haunted;
By fairies, bogles, and banshees,
That roam at night among the trees,
But Ringlin had no fear of these,
        He is not easily daunted.

His limbs were tired the hour was late,
His need of sleep was very great,
It seemed a cosy place to wait,
        The appearance of the morn;
And so he clambered up the height,
And found a shelter for the night,
Where fairy flowers were gleaming white,
        In the shadow of a thorn.

When he was sleeping sound and well,
The fairies entered through a dell,
And I will now proceed to tell,
        Of the revelling so gay.
It was their custom to resort,
At midnight to this lonely fort,
To pass the hours in merry sport,
        Till the dawning of the day.

But much amazed to hear a snore,
For no man ever came before,
At night to sleep in or explore,
        That very uncanny scene;
With joy they all resolved to play,
A prank on Ringlin where he lay,
But none could settle on a way,
        So they left it to their Queen.

Who mixed with other things unknown,
A powder made from witch's bone,
With water in a hollow stone,
   An orphan's tear including;
She gently poured some on his eyes,
And then commanded him to rise,
Which Ringlin did in great surprise,
   To see what was intruding.

The charm made him a fairy small,
And through the grass so thick and tall,
To move or walk without a fall,
   He had the greatest bother;
But soon sweet music filled the air,
And banished all his great despair,
It made him dance o'er brake and briar,
   As light as any other.

Oh! never did so rare a sight,
Appear to mortal eyes at night,
The fort all glowed with magic light,
   And the wind sung melodies;
And as the fairies danced around,
They scarcely seemed to touch the ground,
So full of grace was every bound,
   As they winded through the trees.

And Ringlin's heart was overjoyed,
For he was dancing round beside,
A fairy maid who was the pride,
   Of all that airy throng;
And then a harper took his stand,
The greatest bard in Fairyland,
He played the harp with skilful hand,
   While the others sang this song.

"Let us gaily dance and sing,
Round and round our dewy ring,
For we have no power to stay,
Longer than the dawn of day.
Oh! a merry life is ours,
Dancing round among the flowers,
When the dew is gleaming bright,
In the pale moon's dreamy light".

And when the dance began to pall,
The fairy Queen did loudly call,
A mighty feast appeared for all,
        On a giant paddock stool;
Most happy in his fairy state,
Now Ringlin sat and laughed and ate,
Said he, "Young fellows this is great,
        Who denies that is a fool".

For they had bum-bee bacon there,
All cooked with nicety and care,
And other dishes rich and rare,
        The wine in bluebell glasses;
And while they emptied all the plates,
He spent the time in long debates,
In ridiculing magistrates,
        And all the higher classes.

He told how he was put in jail,
Because he only did regale,
Himself with whisky, beer and ale,
        Such harmless stimulation;
(Alas how fleeting are the joys
That from the use of whisky rise)
The glow of dawn now stained the skies,
        And caused great agitation.

An early cock began to crow,
The fairies knew 'twas time to go,
And vanished quicker than the snow,
        Which falls into a river;
Then Ringlin woke and many groans,
Proclaimed the stiffness of his bones,
'Twas sad to hear his sighs and moans,
        And sad to see him shiver.

To make his misery complete,
A mossy boulder caught his feet,
And in a mire he fell so neat,
        The mud on him cementing;
Then he went home as black as ink,
Filling the air with awful stink,
Resolving never more to drink,
        And loud in his lamenting.   1906

Poem - A STORY PLEASE

On behalf of

John Alexander Stinson
(Grandson of the Poet)
and
Konrad Hugh Alexander Stinson
(Great Grandson of the Poet)

A Story Please

Oh, Grandpa do not light your pipe
But tell us a story please,

So say Heather and little John
When they scramble upon my knees.

I tell them stories of long ago,
Legends and fairy lore,

To the house of dreams and make believe,
I open the golden door.

Jack and the Beanstalk, Puss in Boots,
Snow White and the Wicked Queen,

And how the fairies removed the hump,
From Edmund of the Green.

Hansel and Gretel caught by the Witch,
And pretty Red Riding Hood,

And the birds that covered up with leaves,
The little Babes in the Wood.

How Cinderella went to the Ball and
Rapunzel let down her hair,

And the Beauty who slept a hundred years,
And still kept young and fair.

The Frog Prince and the Golden Ball,
Of the daughter of the King,

And the Children of Laird turned into Swans,
to the Holy Bells would ring.

The Pagan myth of Tirnanogue,
The land of the ever young,

And lost Atlantis earthquake torn,
To the depths of ocean flung.

Such are the tales that I narrate,
To Heather and little John,

And perhaps the children that yet may be,
They shall tell them when I have gone.

1968

Poem - ROSALEEN

On behalf of

Halifax Property Services
18 Main Street, Bangor
Tel. 028 91 463721
Fax. 028 91 450515

Branch Manager:
Lorraine Beatty

Rosaleen

One bright May morning on a hill,
Beside the River Bann;
Amid a grove of shady trees,
My love for her began.
In Ballievey gathering flowers,
That morning she had been;
And that is where I chanced to meet
The blushing Rosaleen.

The birds were fluttering in the trees
As from the scene they fled;
And snowy showers of hawthorn bloom
Descended on her head.
Her arms were full of meadow flowers,
But all their brilliant dyes,
Were pale beside her glowing cheeks,
And dark blue Irish eyes.

Her glossy curls of raven hair
were tossing in the breeze,
Her ruddy lips might fit deceive
The sight of honey bees;
Sure no one knows what beauty is,
If they have never seen,
The girl I met that merry day,
My lovely Rosaleen.

1913

Poem - MOONSHINE

On behalf of

Bangor Steakhouse
119 High Street
Bangor
Co Down
BT20 5BD
Tel. 028 91 470768

Proprietor: J McCormick

Moonshine

· An old fellow of Toombridge was licensed to fish,
in the River Bann and Lough Neagh;
He got a 'still' made and began a new trade,
when fishing for eels did not pay.

The Poteen he made was a powerful stuff,
And cheaper than whisky or gin;
The customers came from all over the place and
lashings of money came in.

Now the Law is severe on people who make
and peddle such liquor for sale,
And Judges are apt to impose heavy fines,
with time for repentance in jail.

That's why the old fellow was greatly perturbed
and shook like a jelly with fright,
When a stern looking Sergeant came to the door
and caught him red-handed one night.

In front of the Sergeant he went on his knees,
for mercy to beg and implore,
And by Joseph and Mary fervently vowed,
"Let me off and I'll do it no more".

"Get up", said the Sergeant, "You've no need to stop,
your arrest is not what I seek.
I simply called to give you an order,
for a couple of bottles a week".

1972

Poem - SEASONS

On behalf of

Mrs Jeanie Thompson

Queen's Parade and Gray's Hill Bangor.   Pre 1899

1999

Seasons

The springtime comes, the leaves and flowers appear

And butterflies and bees pursue again,

Their journeys o'er the meadows and the hills;

The days grow warmer and the bloom appears,

Upon the trees and perfume fills the air.

The birds assume a brighter dress and sound;

Among the woods a louder sweeter song.

Then summer comes and shallow murmuring streams,

Flow on half hidden by the tow'ring sedge,

And o'er the pools and verdure of the bogs,

Flash the clear wings of gorgeous dragon flies.

The juicy fruit gleams on the garden trees

And fields of grain turn yellow and mature,

Beneath the warm benevolence of the sun.

Then autumn comes, the crops are gathered in,

And men rejoice if 'Fortune' has been kind.

It is a pleasant time which is begemmed,

By moonlight that is brightest of the year;

By fresh invigorating misty dawns,

And by sunsets that make more lovely still,

The whisp'ring woods and their decaying leaves.

1909

Poem - HELEN

Dedicated to the late

David Alexander 1902 - 1992

A native of Banbridge, Co Down
who took great pleasure in his brother's verse

On behalf of his family

Helen

Have you ever seen Helen or listened her song,
On a calm summer eve when it echoed along,
From her garden of roses o'er valleys and dells,
By the green shady banks of the Bann where she dwells.

Within sight of the blue misty mountains of Mourne,
And the town of Banbridge; oh, could Nature adorn,
A more exquisite scene with a colleen more fair?
No! the greatest attainment of beauty is there.

Such a blending of mischief and tenderness lies,
In the light of her smile and the blue of her eyes,
And the sound of her laugh is so pleasant to hear,
That no heart could be heavy when Helen is near.

There is nothing on earth that would ever compare,
With the clustering curls of her golden-brown hair,
And no lovelier hue on the clouds is impressed,
When the glory of sunset is gilding the west.

Long long may her blue eyes continue to shine,
Out their beautiful message of love into mine,
And long may the true love that so brightens her smile,
Make a heaven for me of this green-bosomed isle.

1909

Poem - THE KING'S SONG
(On the death of his favourite Bard)

On behalf of

Mrs Edna Linton of Belfast
(Sister of the poet)

The King's Song

On the death of his favourite Bard

Circa 800AD

Your voice that once enraptured me
With all its magic power of sound;
Your songs of love and bravery,
The hills no longer echo round.
Your harp hangs silent on the wall,
I gaze at it through blinding tears,
Oh! how those strings to me recall
The faded joys of other years;
For when you woke the harp to life,
You could lull a babe to sleep,
Could make an army mad for strife,
Or cause them all to sigh and weep.
But death has dimmed your fiery eye,
And hushed the music of your tongue;
Among the heroes now you lie,
Of whom in other days you sung.
And now your strain shall thrill no more
My heart in war or banquet hall;
Our days of friendship too are o'er,
Which I had valued more than all.
Sleep in peace! you cannot see,
The gloom that falls on Erin's Isle;
The stranger comes to bind the free,
To steal, to murder, and defile.
To Godless foreign foes a prey,
Her glorious day is nearly run;
A thousand years shall pass away
Before the rising of her sun!

1910

My Ireland

From this far distant region in which I sojourn,
To my own native Ireland in dreams I return,
And my sorrows all flee when I look at the smile,
Of the sun on the hills of that evergreen isle.

And I see mid the gloom of the woods the bright gleams,
Of the lakes and the far flowing musical streams,
And a thousand wild valleys and scenes that I knew,
In the days of my boyhood appear to my view.

And many a pathway I journey until,
I can see the old home on the side of the hill,
And pass through the gateway and hear the sweet sound,
Of the voices of loved ones come floating around.

But the vision soon fades and I waken to sigh,
As I hear the loud voice of the wind rushing by,
And the roar of the waves as they fall in the bay,
For I know that the old home is far far away.

1925

Impromptu Lines On Pigs

A fearsome man was the Butcher when he took the Porker's life,
What brains it had he dundered in, then stuck in its throat the knife.
On the palpitating carcass, hot water he poured with care,
Then with a big broad scraper he ripped off the skin and hair.

The farmer's wife got the liver and the fat for melting down;
The Farmer got drunk as usual and the Butcher half-a-crown.
The dogs got puddings to fight for, the bladder I claimed as mine;
So ended a day of pleasure for all but the luckless Swine.

Now the Jews are a foolish people, they never throw in the pan,
A piece of the greatest blessing that was ever known to man.
But I have a wiser doctrine, the Pig is a beast I adore,
Belly or back, it's all the same, I eat it and ask for more.

I like to eat ham or bacon with my cabbage, beans or peas,
And I would not turn my nose up at ham knobs or pickled knees.

When next you walk in Cromac Street be observant as you go,
You'll see good bacon hung on hooks in many a salty row.
And smoked or green, fat striped or lean, each chunk of bacon you see,
Are silent sad memorials of poor Pigs that used to be.

Imagine you see them lying in their sties so snug and warm,
Their only pleasure food and sleep, with no fear of any harm.
Then think of the heartless farmer bending down in the gloom,
To see if they've reached the limit on his knotted string of doom.

Then drop a tear of compassion and your thanks unstinted give,
To our humble friends the Porkers who must die that me may live.

1935

The Toothache

What makes us loudly curse and swear
What makes us rave and pull our hair
What torment is the worst to bear
      The toothache!

What makes the children roar and weep
What makes the gossips silent keep
What robs us of our precious sleep
      The toothache!

What makes the coolest temper hot
What makes a hollow cheek grow fat
What makes us want to kick the cat
      The toothache!

What makes us wild and wakeful lie
While midnight hours go slowly by
And almost wish that we could die
      The toothache!

What gives some people such a thirst
What punishment would be the worst
Down in the land of the accursed
      The toothache!

1910

A Household Hint

To those who wish to save their coals,
I recommend the plan,
Invented by Scrapeha'penny,
Who was a very clever man.

No fire except for cookery,
Did in his house appear,
And even so he still complained,
That fuel was too dear.

In summer and in winter time,
His rule was still the same,
For when the cold was sharp enough,
To chill his hardy frame.

He simply slung a bag of coals,
Upon his back and then,
He hauled it up and down the stairs,
Till he was warm again.

1908

Poem- COMING HOME

On behalf of

Ruth Alexander
(Grand-daughter of the Poet)

'For Dad'

Purdysburn Village, County Down.
Drawn by Heather Victoria Stinson
(Grand-daughter of the Poet)

Coming Home

There's a little Irish Village
and they call it Purdysburn,
Where a little boy with ginger hair
is awaiting my return.

And a loving wife and daughter
will fondly greet me there,
And have such tales to tell me
as we sit around the fire.

How lovely is the village
in the early morning light,
When I see it after sailing
upon the sea all night.

And the boy will run to meet me
and the first thing he will say,
Is, "Daddy, tell me Daddy
have you come back to stay?"

Oh, its good to stay where you belong
but its only those who roam,
Who ever know the pleasure
and the joy of coming home.

1946

The Clergy and Select Vestry of Saint Comgall's Parish Church
sincerely appreciate the financial help afforded by the following:

Ailsa Lodge Nursing Home - Bangor

Allen: E, Insurance Broker - Belfast

Alexander: Harold R

Alexander: David T

Alexander: Ruth

A.S.K. Electrical Limited - Bangor

Bangor Steak House - Bangor: J McCormick

Battersea Guest House - Bangor: John and Rene Brann

Benmore Courtyard Cottages - Olga & Neil Rogers

Boland Reilly Homes Ltd - Bangor

Brown: Billy, Barber - Bangor

Burns: David, Butcher - Bangor

Campbell: Gillian, Estate Agent - Bangor

Clandeboye

Coey: Alastair, Architect

Davidson: Joan - Carrickfergus

Down Diving Services - Bangor: Stanley McKeown

Elizabeth's Florist - Bangor: Elizabeth McBurney

Emery: Minnie - England

Essentially Yours, Fragrant Oils - Bangor

Gorman: Sir John

Halifax Property Services - Bangor

Hawthorn: Norman - Belfast

Hunter: Mary Ann - Bangor

Hylands Developments Ltd - Belfast

Linton: Edna - Belfast

Meridian Beauty Salon - Bangor

The McBride Family

McClure: Mervyn

McDowell: Christine and Ronnie

McGowan: Nigel P, Kitchen Furniture Design & Manufacturers - Killinchy

McVeigh: Winnie - Bangor

N & N Cheque Encashment Centre - Bangor: Sam Collins

NN Motors - Bangor: Noel Mutch

Ovis Video Installation - Bangor: Norman Taylor and Tom Smyth

PropertyNews - Portadown

Newberry: Robert, Plumbing and Heating - Bangor

Russells of Bangor, Funeral Directors - Bangor

Sammy Mellon & Sons Ltd. - Bangor

Sinclair: Elizabeth - Belfast

Sony Centre - Belfast

Stewart: David and Linda - Lisburn

Stewart: Claire and Martin - Bangor

Stinson: John Alexander - Belfast

Stuart: Anita - Enniskillen

Thompson: Jeanie - Bangor

Ulster Property Sales - Bangor

W J L Photography - Bangor